BOJUTSU

HANBO, ROKUSHAKU-BO AND JO

BUJINKAN TECHNIQUE REFERENCE SERIES

DUNCAN MITCHELL

BUDO DOKOKAI (BRISBANE, AUSTRALIA)

Disclaimer: This book is presented as a reference guide only. Nothing described in this book should be practised or undertaken without the personal guidance of a suitably qualified and experienced martial arts instructor. Furthermore, a physician should be first consulted before deciding whether or not to attempt any of the techniques described. The author and publisher accept no responsibility whatsoever for any injury that may result from practising the techniques and/or instructions within. This book is presented only as a means of preserving a unique aspect of the heritage of the martial arts, and neither the author nor publisher makes any representation, guarantee or warranty that any technique or instruction described within will be safe or effective in any self-defence situation. In addition, specific martial arts techniques detailed in these pages may not be justified in any particular situation or applicable under local, state or federal laws. Neither the publisher nor the author makes any representation or warranty regarding the legality or appropriateness of any technique mentioned in this book.

Written and Illustrated by Duncan Mitchell

Published by the Budō Dōkōkai, Brisbane, Australia.

www.budodokokai.com

ISBN 978-0-6489608-2-9 (Paperback)

ISBN 978-0-6489608-3-6 (ebook)

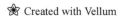 Created with Vellum

For Yoshie

CONTENTS

PART I
HANBŌJUTSU
半棒術

PART II
ROKUSHAKU-BŌJUTSU
六尺棒術

PART III
JŌJUTSU
杖術

OUR LEGACY

The Bujinkan is the martial arts organisation formed by Masaaki Hatsumi-sensei to propagate the essence of the nine Ryūha (traditional schools of martial arts) of which he inherited the title of Sōke (grandmaster).

- 神伝不動流打拳体術 Shinden Fudō Ryū Daken Taijutsu
- 九鬼神伝流八法秘剣術 Kuki Shinden Ryū Happō Biken-Jutsu
- 高木揚心流柔体術 Takagi Yōshin Ryū Jūtai-Jutsu
- 玉虎流骨指術 Gyokko Ryū Kosshi-Jutsu
- 虎倒流骨法術 Kotō Ryū Koppō-Jutsu
- 義鑑流骨法術 Gikan Ryū Koppō-Jutsu
- 玉心流骨法術 Gyokushin Ryū Koppō-Jutsu
- 戸隠流忍法体術 Togakure Ryū Ninpō Taijutsu
- 雲隠流忍法体術 Kumogakure Ryū Ninpō Taijutsu

The Bujinkan has its headquarters in Noda City, Japan and has spread internationally since its formation in 1968; now encompassing thousands of students worldwide.

It is the Bujinkan's training philosophy of moving away from the *form* of techniques and developing one's response in accordance with the situation that brings forth a heightened awareness and a dynamic martial art.

高松寿嗣 Toshitsugu Takamatsu - Teacher of the Bujinkan Founder Masaaki Hatsumi

Toshitsugu Takamatsu was born in 1888 and from the age of nine was schooled daily in the martial arts that he later would inherit as grandmaster.

Initially, he trained in Kōbe under the tutelage of Toda Shinryuken Masamitsu and then in the Dōjō of Mizuta Yoshitaro Tadafusa. Later he moved to the nearby town of Akashi with his father, where he trained under Ishitani Matsutaro Tagekage.

In 1912, Takamatsu travelled to China where he lived until his return to Japan in 1919. In China, he headed the "Nippon Minkoku Seinen Butou-kai" martial arts organisation. He was also involved in many incidents that had him fighting for his life. It was during this period that he became known as Mōko no Tora (The Mongolian Tiger).

In 1957, Takamatsu-sensei took on a young Masaaki Hatsumi as his student and successor. From that point on, Takamatsu-sensei would devote his time through training and writing to pass on the nine schools and his greater vision of Budō to his student.

初見良昭 Masaaki Hatsumi - Bujinkan Founder

Born in 1931 in Noda City, Japan, Masaaki Hatsumi-sensei spent his youth training in several martial arts, amongst which he was highly accomplished in Jūdō, Karate, Kendō, Aikidō, and Western boxing.

Immediately after the Second World War, he was assigned to teach Jūdō at an American Air Force base near Tokyo. It was here that he realised that, since the Japanese martial arts had modernised into competitive sports, the larger and more athletic Americans could achieve in a very short time what would take the smaller Japanese years of study. It was then that Hatsumi-sensei set himself to search for the true Japanese martial arts of ancient Japan.

His search led him to a martial artist from Nara in the west of Japan named Toshitsugu Takamatsu.

From his first encounter at age 27, Hatsumi-sensei regularly took the night train on Saturday evening to arrive on Sunday morning for his apprenticeship in the nine martial art lineages he would later inherit as grandmaster. Hatsumi-sensei continued his training for fifteen years until Takamatsu-sensei's death in 1972.

Combining the essence of the teachings from Takamatsu, Hatsumi-sensei established the Bujinkan Dōjō.

Masaaki Hatsumi has served as an advisor for many movies, television shows and theatre productions since the 1960s, such as "Shinobi no Mono", "Kage no Gundan", and "You Only Live Twice". He even had an acting role as "Yamaji Tetzuzan" in the children's TV series "Sekai Ninja-sen Jiraya" (Jiraya and the World Ninja War).

Hatsumi-sensei is the author of many books in both English and Japanese and has produced a series of DVDs demonstrating the martial arts of the Bujinkan.

From 1986 to 2003, he travelled the world conducting seminars where five hundred to a thousand enthusiasts would gather to train together at one time.

Due to his work spreading Japan's true martial arts around the world, Masaaki Hatsumi has received numerous awards, including being the first martial artist to receive the International Culture Award from the emperor of Japan.

Hatsumi-sensei retired from active training in 2020 at the age of 88.

INTRODUCTION

Bōjutsu, the art of using the Bō (staff), is a core element of the traditional Japanese martial arts. In the Bujinkan, training in Bōjutsu includes the Rokushaku-Bō (long staff), Hanbō (half-staff), and Jō (walking staff/cane).

Taijutsu (body technique) is the foundation of the Bujinkan martial arts; however, unlike sporting contests, actual combat is not about facing an opponent under equal conditions; it requires us to defeat the opponent by any means necessary, where losing could result in severe injury or death. Additionally, as we age, physical decline is inevitable. Therefore, the notion that a martial artist should always engage an opponent unarmed, especially in unequal situations such as facing an armed attacker, multiple opponents, or a much stronger adversary, is unrealistic.

One of the fundamental aspects of being human is our ability to utilise tools. Even prehistoric humans instinctively picked up sticks or stones to defend themselves. In the Bujinkan, weapon techniques are seen as extensions of Taijutsu, transforming everyday objects into effective weapons. Bōjutsu embodies this philosophy, allowing items such as canes or umbrellas to be used as weapons, all while grounded in the basics of Taijutsu. This adaptability empowers us to defend ourselves in various situations.

In Bōjutsu, the staff is not seen as an external object but as an extension of one's body. The Bō moves in harmony with us as we skillfully manage its balance, centre of gravity, and length. Like a dance partner, the staff follows our lead. It is essential not to cling to the weapon or let it dominate our mental focus; practice should continue until the Bō becomes an integral part of us, seamlessly incorporated without being the focal point of our conscious intention.

The first stage is to ground oneself in the basic kata of Bōjutsu, repeating the exercises repeatedly until they become ingrained in the body. Establishing a good foundation requires a high degree of precision and accuracy in training. Next, one must release from the form of the technique and internalise its feelings and principles.

My purpose in writing this book is to provide both new and experienced Bujinkan students with a simple reference guide to the basic techniques of Bōjutsu. This volume brings the Kata for Rokushaku-Bō, Hanbō, and Jō together in one convenient resource.

This book is not intended as a "how-to" or "teach-yourself" guide to Bōjutsu. I believe that martial arts can only be studied correctly under the guidance of an experienced instructor. As such, I have avoided overly detailed technique descriptions and illustrations, providing just enough detail for the book to be helpful as a reference guide.

How to Use This Book

This book is divided into three parts:

- **Part One: Hanbōjutsu** (half-staff)
- **Part Two: Rokushaku-Bōjutsu** (long staff)
- **Part Three: Jōjutsu** (walking staff/cane)

I should make clear that this book is not a literal translation of the Densho* but my description of the basic technique and Kata. In researching this book, I have reviewed original Japanese handwritten documents, books,

---

* 伝書 Densho: Scrolls of transmission of the secrets for the art.

and DVDs produced by Hatsumi-sensei, my training notes, and my study with various Japanese teachers over the years.

In writing the Kata, I have outlined the basic forms as simply as possible and avoided nuanced terms, histories, philosophical ideas and differences between the schools.

Hatsumi-sensei suggested that Kata should not be read as a set of instructions but as a story or history retold from one generation to the next. To practice the Kata is to retell the tale and walk for a moment on the path of our ancestors in the art. In keeping with this feeling, I have described each Kata in the first person.

It should be noted that different teachers in Japan have diverse and contradictory interpretations of how basic techniques and Kata are performed. Rather than listing all the conflicting views and variations, I presented a singular version of each technique that I feel most closely represents the basic form. It should, therefore, be noted that this book is only a reference guide and that instruction from your teacher should always take precedence over any description or illustration provided in this book.

Finally, I would like to express my sincere hope that this book provides you, the reader, with some guidance and direction on the rewarding and lifelong journey of Japanese Budō.

Please feel free to contact me with any suggestions, corrections and requests for future editions of this book.

www.budodokokai.com

budodokokai@gmail.com

PART I
HANBŌJUTSU
半棒術

CHAPTER 1
HANBŌ (HALF-STAFF)
半棒

The Hanbō ("half staff"), alternatively referred to as Sanjakubō ("3-shaku staff")[*], is a hardwood stick measuring half the length of the Rokushaku-Bō ("6-shaku staff")[†].

The Keiko Gata[‡] of the Kukishin Ryū forms the basis of Hanbō-jutsu in the Bujinkan. The weapon is then applied within variations of the basic Taijutsu techniques of each Ryūha[§].

The distancing of Hanbō-jutsu closely mirrors that of Taijutsu. The opponent's attack is first evaded, then followed up with the stick being used to strike, thrust or employed in Gyaku-Waza[#], Nage-Waza[°], or Shime-Waza[**].

The Hanbō can also be adapted to sword techniques. This principle is encapsulated in the secret teaching of "the stick becomes a sword".

The Hanbō lends itself well to self-defence applications, in which the

---

[*] 三尺 3-shaku = 90.9cm
[†] 六尺 6-shaku = 181.8cm
[‡] 稽古型 Keiko Gata: practice forms
[§] 流派 Ryūha: Schools (of Martial Arts)
[#] 逆技 Gyaku-Waza: joint locking techniques
[°] 投技 Nage-Waza: throwing techniques
[**] 絞め技 Shime-Waza: constriction techniques

weapon can be substituted for everyday items such as a walking stick, umbrella, pool cue, or golf club. In addition to practising the historical forms, it is essential to occasionally incorporate such everyday items into your training to reinforce your understanding of real-world applications.

History

Various legends are attributed to the formation of Hanbōjutsu from the Kukishin Ryū.

One tale suggests its development from an ancient weapon: a stone ring mounted on the end of a stick and utilised as a club or mace in combat. Another legend attributes the foundation of Hanbō-jutsu to an incident of a spear being cleaved in half on the battlefield and the remaining length of the shaft being repurposed to defeat an adversary.

Although once there were most probably specific techniques for clubs and maces, and there may have been techniques for using weapons that have been broken in combat, the current repertoire of Kata we observe today likely emerged not for battlefield application but for use by travellers as a weapon of self-defence during the relatively tranquil years of the Edo Period (1603 - 1868).

Similar to the Jō, the status of the Hanbō likely ascended beyond its role as a minor weapon in the Edo period, evolving into a more significant area of study from the late 19th century. Unlike traditional samurai weapons such as the spear, naginata and sword, the Hanbō has a more immediately practical application as a modern self-defence tool, as the weapon can be easily substituted for various everyday items one may carry.

Hanbō Dimensions

In the Bujinkan, the standard length for the Hanbō is 3-shaku (90.9cm). However, many practitioners find this traditional length too short and opt to customise the dimensions to their height, crafting a Hanbō tailored to measure from the floor to the level of their belt. This personalised style is known as a Koshikiri-Bō ("Waist Cut Stick").

Hanbō can be crafted from any suitable hardwood, with historical preferences being either Akagashi (Japanese Red Oak) or Shirakashi (Japanese White Oak). The preferred diameter is typically 1-sun (3 cm), though individuals with smaller hands may opt for a smaller diameter of 8-bu (2.4cm).

In addition to practising with a wooden stick, a soft training Hanbō can be fashioned using a conduit core padded with pipe insulation and wrapped in vinyl, leather or cloth duct tape. This soft training tool allows you to strike through your target and commit to the techniques while providing a higher level of safety.

Power Generation

Ken Tai Ichi-Jo ("the strike and the body as one") is an important principle that emphasises using your entire body to generate power, which is transferred through the Hanbō. Rather than swinging the stick with your hands, you use synchronised body movement to deliver the maximum force through the weapon.

Central to effective power delivery is maintaining your elbows relatively close to your body and preventing them from flaring out as you manoeuvre the stick. Mastery of this principle hinges on practice until you can seamlessly transfer power through the Hanbō via the sequential and coordinated action of the foot, spine, hand, and bō.

It is essential always to maintain a light grip on the Hanbō and allow the weapon to slide freely through your hands. This will keep your arms free of tension and facilitate the effective transmission of power from the body's movement. The grip on the Hanbō should be as delicate as if cradling quails' eggs. This light touch ensures that the flow of power remains unimpeded. By adhering to this principle, practitioners can fully capitalise on the body's kinetic energy in power delivery.

Morote Nage (also known as Awase Nage) is an effective exercise for instilling the basic principles of maintaining a light grip, fluid body movement, and coordinated action. If tension is present in your body during Morote Nage, your opponent's body will naturally respond by resisting the force, rendering your attempt to throw ineffective. Only correct alignment and the transfer of power will work effectively.

諸手投 Morote Nage

1. I hold the Hanbō near its centre with my right hand (palm up) and the rear end of the stick against my body with my left hand (palm down). The opponent mirrors my posture.

2. I place my left foot forward as I transfer my weight across and raise the rear end of the stick by rolling my left shoulder blade.

3. Using the opponent's right hand as the fulcrum, I place my right foot forward, transfer my weight, and roll the stick over in a big arc by rolling my right shoulder blade. My grip remains very soft on the Hanbō.

4. The opponent's balance is rocked back evenly on his heels, preventing him from taking a backward step and causing him to fall.

仕込み杖 Shikomi-Zue ("Prepared Cane")

In addition to the standard Hanbō, a blade may be concealed within the stick. This style of weapon is called Shikomi-Zue ("prepared cane"). The Shikomi-Zue became well known in Japan through movies about the fictional character Zatoichi, a blind swordsman who famously wields this weapon.

仕込み杖 *Shikomi-Zue*

The blade of the Shikomi-Zue is typically shorter (around two Shaku or 60cm long) and much thinner than the standard Katana. So, unlike in the movies, rather than wielding the Shikomi-Zue as a sword against a sword-wielding opponent, the weapon should rather be wielded as a Hanbō, with its blade sheathed, until the opponent is disarmed and/or put under control. The thin blade can then be drawn within the flow of the movement, used to slash targets such as the wrist or neck or thrust into the opponent.

In the Bujinkan, there are no formal Kata for Shikomi-Zue. Instead, the practitioners learn to use the weapon through direct instruction from their teacher (Kuden) and their creativity in adapting traditional techniques and applications (Henka).

The most common style of Shikomi-Zue is the sword cane, but other variations exist. Some Shikomi-Zue have a knife concealed in the handle, while others contain a weighted chain running inside the stick.

CHAPTER 2
HANBŌ: SANSHIN NO KAMAE
三心の構

The Kamae* of weapons such as Ken (sword), Yari (spear) or Naginata (glaive/halberd) are designed to physically position you for the weapon's practical use in battle.

This differs from Hanbō in that its Kamae are outwardly natural while internally positioning you in the correct state of mind.

This is known as the "Kamae of no Kamae".

Physically, the Sanshin no Kamae teach natural, efficient and balanced body configuration. The Kamae allows you to maintain a body structure that is both manoeuvrable and stable. Stability will enable you to keep yourself in balance and deliver attacks from a strong base. Manoeuvrability will allow you to avoid your opponent's attacks and to close in quickly to counterattack.

Similarly, the Sanshin no Kamae maintain a mental state that is both manoeuvrable and stable. Stability comes from the solid mental state of standing naturally but intentionally. They are postures devoid of aggression or fear. Manoeuvrability comes from the mental state of your conscious awareness surrounding you and the ability to respond naturally to any attack.

---

* 構 Kamae: body structure/stance

型破りの構 Kata-Yaburi no Kamae

Also known as 平一文字の構 *Hira Ichimonji no Kamae.*

I stand in Shizentai ("natural posture"). My arms hang straight down, and I hold the Hanbō horizontally in front of me with my hands shoulder-width apart.

型破構 *Kata-Yaburi no Kamae*

無念無想の構 Munen Musō no Kamae

Also known as 楯の構 *Tate no Kamae.*

I stand in Shizentai. I hold the Hanbō vertically, like a walking stick, in either my right or left hand.

無念無想の構 *Munen Musō no Kamae*

Alternatively, the Hanbō can be carried as illustrated.

無念無想の構 *Munen Musō no Kamae (alternative)*

音無しの構 Otonashi no Kamae

This posture is the opposite of Kata-Yaburi no Kamae.

I stand in Shizentai. My arms hang straight down, holding the Hanbō horizontally behind my back with my hands shoulder-width apart.

音無しの構 *Otonashi no Kamae*

CHAPTER 3
HANBŌ: KIHON GATA 1
基本型その一

1. すくい打ち Sukui Uchi

1. From Kata-Yaburi no Kamae, I step forward with my left foot as I slide the Hanbō through my hands to strike upwards from below with the left end of the stick.

2. I return to Kata-Yaburi no Kamae, then repeat the technique on the right side.

2. 反返し打ち Han-Kaeshi Uchi

1. From Kata-Yaburi no Kamae, I step back diagonally to my left with my left foot, release my left hand, and turn the Hanbō over half a rotation with

my right hand. I catch the right end of the Hanbō with my left hand as I bend my knees and sink my weight to strike down.

2. I return to Kata-Yaburi no Kamae, then repeat the technique on the right side.

3. 片手振り Katate Furi

1. From Kata-Yaburi no Kamae, I step back to Yoko Ichimonji no Kamae with my right foot.

2. I then change the grip of my right hand from behind my right thigh (out of view of the opponent) so that my palm is facing out.

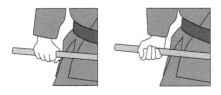

3. I release my left hand and advance one step forward with my right foot as I swing the rear end of the Hanbō around to deliver a strike to the left side of the opponent's head.

4. I return to Kata-Yaburi no Kamae, then repeat the technique on the left side.

4. 八字片手振り Hachiji Katate Furi

1. From Munen Musō no Kamae, I advance with my right foot as I swing the Hanbō in a large, continuous figure-eight motion in front of me.

2. I return to Munen Musō no Kamae and repeat the technique on the left side.

[Note: The figure-eight swing is not done with the action of the wrist but generated from the body. Practice advancing and retreating while swinging the Hanbō continuously and striking down at the opponent from within the flow.]

5. 突き返し Tsuki Kaeshi

1. From Munen Musō no Kamae, I advance with my right foot, placing the Hanbō under my right armpit. Then, I use my right hand to thrust forward with the top of the stick.

2. I then grasp the Hanbō from under my right armpit with my left hand and step forward with my left foot, delivering a horizontal strike to the right side of the opponent's head with the rear end of the stick.

3. I release my right hand and turn the Hanbō over half a rotation with my left hand to catch the left end of the Hanbō with my right hand and strike down to the top of the opponent's head.

4. I return to Munen Musō no Kamae and repeat the technique on the left side.

6. 突き胴振り Tsuki Dō-Furi

1. From Munen Musō no Kamae, I advance with my right foot, place the Hanbō under my right armpit, and use my right hand to thrust forward with the top of the stick.

2. I then grasp the end of the Hanbō with my left hand and deliver a horizontal strike to the left side of the opponent's head with the rear end of the stick.

3. I return to Munen Musō no Kamae and repeat the technique on the left side.

7. 片手振り面打ち Katate Furi Men Uchi

1. From Munen Musō no Kamae, I advance with my right foot as I swing the bottom end of the Hanbō to strike upwards from below.

2. I then grasp the end of the Hanbō with my left hand and slide my right hand down the stick to deliver a downward strike to the top of the opponent's head.

3. I return to Munen Musō no Kamae and repeat the technique on the left side.

8. 栗返し Kuri Kaeshi

1. From Otonashi no Kamae, I step diagonally forward with my right foot as I rotate the right end of the Hanbō with my right wrist, as illustrated, without breaking my right-hand grip, to bring it to the back of my right shoulder.

2. I then release my left hand and use my right hand to deliver a downward strike with the rear end of the Hanbō.

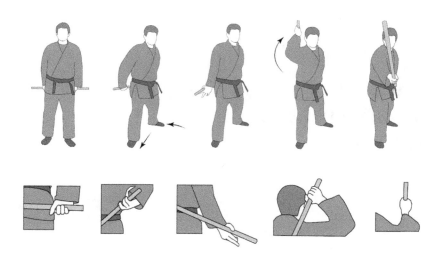

3. I return to Otonashi no Kamae. Then, repeat the technique on the left side.

[Note: For those lacking shoulder and wrist flexibility to perform the basic technique, the stick may be rolled between the index and middle finger, as illustrated below.]

栗返し *Kuri Kaeshi (alternative)*

CHAPTER 4
HANBŌ: KIHON GATA 2
基本型その二

1. 片胸捕 Kata Mune Dori

1. From Munen Musō no Kamae, the opponent grabs my left lapel with their right hand.

2. I slide my right hand down the stick and rotate it over the opponent's right wrist from below.

3. I grasp the end of the stick with my left hand from below to firmly capture their wrist.

4. I shift forward to unbalance the opponent backward on their heels.

5. I then step back with my left foot and drop to my left knee as I rotate to my left, causing the opponent to fall on their back.

6. I return to Munen Musō no Kamae and repeat the technique on the left side.

2. 両胸捕 Ryō Mune Dori

1. From Munen Musō no Kamae, the opponent grabs both my lapels.

2. I slide my right hand down the stick and rotate it over the opponent's wrists from below.

3. I grasp the end of the stick with my left hand from below to firmly capture their wrists.

4. I shift forward to unbalance the opponent backward on their heels.

5. I then step back with my left foot and drop to my left knee as I rotate to my left, causing the opponent to fall on their back.

6. I return to Munen Musō no Kamae and repeat the technique on the left side.

3. 水車 Suisha

1. From Munen Musō no Kamae, the opponent grabs both my lapels.

2. I slide my right hand down the stick and rotate it over the opponent's right wrist from below.

3. I grasp the end of the stick with my left hand from below to firmly capture their right wrist.

4. I lower my hips and twist my spine to my left as I push downward to break their right-hand grip.

5. Next, I release my right-hand grip on the stick, rotate it above the opponent's left wrist with my left hand, and retake the right end of the stick with my right hand.

6. I then drop my hips as I strike down on the opponent's left wrist with the middle of the Hanbō, breaking their left-hand grip on my lapel.

7. I return to Munen Musō no Kamae and repeat the technique on the left side.

4. 片手捕 Kata Te Dori

1. From Munen Musō no Kamae, the opponent grabs my right wrist with their left hand.

2. I slide my right hand down the stick and rotate it to the outside of the opponent's left wrist from below.

3. I grasp the end of the stick with my left hand from above and shift forward to unbalance the opponent backward on their heels.

4. I then step diagonally back with my left foot as I rotate to my left, putting pressure on the back of the opponent's hand and either causing them to break their grip on my wrist or fall down in front of me.

5. I return to Munen Musō no Kamae and repeat the technique on the left side.

5. 両手捕 Ryō Te Dori

1. From Munen Musō no Kamae, the opponent grabs both my wrists.

2. I slide my right hand down the stick as I step in with my right foot and turn with the feeling of driving my right elbow towards the opponent and breaking my wrist out of the space between their thumb and index finger in the direction of my thumb. I rotate the right end of the stick over the opponent's right wrist from below.

3. I then grasp the end of the stick with my left hand from below to firmly capture their wrist and shift forward to unbalance the opponent backward on their heels.

4. Next, I step back with my right foot as I rotate to my right, putting pressure on the back of the opponent's right hand and either causing them to break their grip on my wrist or fall down in front of me.

5. I return to Munen Musō no Kamae and repeat the technique on the left side.

6. 鬼砕 Oni Kudaki

1. From Munen Musō no Kamae, the opponent attacks with a straight right punch to the face.

2. I step diagonally backward to my right and parry the attack with my left arm as I slide my right hand down to the middle of the stick.

3. I hinge forward and pass the stick under the opponent's right upper arm from below while grasping the top of the stick with my left hand.

4. I then step forward with my left foot as I rotate my left shoulder towards the opponent to bend their right arm and apply the lock.

5. Holding their wrist firmly in the lock, I shift forward and apply pressure down with my left hand and up with my right, causing the opponent to fall on their back.

6. I return to Munen Musō no Kamae and repeat the technique on the left side.

7. 胴締 Dō Jime

1. From Munen Musō no Kamae, the opponent grabs both my lapels and rotates their right hip deeply for a hip throw.

2. I block the throw by pushing my hip against them and sinking my weight downwards as I pass the stick across their body and grasp the opposite end with my left hand.

3. I then push the middle of the stick firmly against the opponent's ribs and step back with my left foot as I turn my body, causing them to fall on their back.

4. I return to Munen Musō no Kamae and repeat the technique on the left side.

8. 弁慶捕 Benkei Dori

1. From Munen Musō no Kamae, the opponent steps in deeply with their right foot and attempts to apply Kannuki-Jime (bear hug) from behind.

2. Before the opponent can establish their grip, I step my right foot diagonally back, drop my hips, and extend my arms out to either side.

3. I bend forward to slide the stick behind the opponent's right ankle and grasp the opposite end with my left hand.

4. I sink my weight back as I pull their leg forward, causing the opponent to fall on their back.

5. I return to Munen Musō no Kamae and repeat the technique on the left side.

9. 棒返 Bō Gaeshi

1. From Munen Musō no Kamae, the opponent grabs the end of my stick with their left hand.

2. I raise the rear end of the stick and hold it against my body with my left hand.

3. I then rotate the right end of the stick in a tight arc to apply Hon Gyaku to the opponent's wrist.

4. Once the lock is applied, I step in with either my right or left foot, causing the opponent to fall.

5. I return to Munen Musō no Kamae and repeat the technique on the left side.

[Note: This technique can be repeated by rotating the opponent's wrist into Omote Gyaku, Ura Gyaku, or Take-Ori and stepping in to throw.]

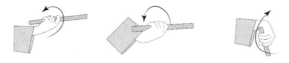

棒返 *Bō Gaeshi Variations: Omote Gyaku, Ura Gyaku, Take Ori*

CHAPTER 5
HANBŌ: SHODEN NO KATA
初傳之型

片手折 *Katate Ori: Striking the outside of the opponent's left elbow joint with the middle of the stick, breaking their grip on my lapel.*

片手折 Katate Ori

I am in Kata-Yaburi no Kamae.

1. The opponent grabs my right lapel with their left hand and prepares to stab with a Shōtō* in their right hand.
2. I step back diagonally to my right with my left foot.
3. Holding the Hanbō horizontally, I strike the outside of the

_____

* 小刀 Shōtō: short sword or knife

opponent's left elbow joint with the middle of the stick, breaking their grip on my lapel.

突落 Tsuki Otoshi

I am in Kata-Yaburi no Kamae.

1. The opponent grabs my right lapel with their left hand and prepares to stab a Shōtō in their right hand.
2. I step back diagonally to my right with my left foot.
3. Holding the Hanbō horizontally, I strike the outside of the opponent's left elbow joint with the middle of the stick, breaking their grip on my lapel.
4. I release my left-hand grip on the stick, turn the Hanbō over, and thrust the stick directly at the opponent's face.

打技 Uchi Waza

I am in Kata-Yaburi no Kamae.

1. The opponent attacks with a right-hand stab at my stomach with a Shōtō.
2. I evade by stepping back diagonally to my left with my left foot.
3. I release my left hand and turn the Hanbō over, using the left end of the stick to strike down from above at the opponent's right wrist.
4. I then slide my right hand up the Hanbō, release my left hand, and swing the rear end of the stick around in a big arc to strike the left side of the opponent's head.

流捕 Nagare Dori

I am in Kata-Yaburi no Kamae.

1. The opponent attacks with a right-hand stab at my stomach with a Shōtō.

2. I evade by stepping back diagonally to my right with my right foot as I grasp the opponent's right wrist with my left hand.
3. I place the left end of the Hanbō behind the opponent's right hip. I then rotate my right wrist as I lift my right hand to put the right end of the stick to their upper right arm.
4. I step back diagonally to my right with my left foot, so a lock is applied with the Hanbō between the opponent's hip and upper arm.
5. The opponent falls on their back.
6. Finally, I strike to the point Wakitsubo (under the armpit) with the end of the stick.

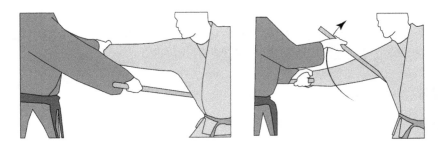

流捕 *Nagare Dori: Applying a lock between the rear of the opponent's hip and upper arm. Also known as Koshi-Ori.*

霞掛 Kasumi Gake

I am in Kata-Yaburi no Kamae.

1. The opponent attacks with a right-hand stab at my stomach with a Shōtō.
2. I evade the attack by stepping to my left with my left foot, turning to my right, and grasping the opponent's right wrist with my right hand.
3. I then place the right end of the Hanbō in front of the opponent's right hip, rotate my left wrist as I lift my left hand, and place the left end of the stick on their upper right arm.
4. I step to my right with my right foot and apply a lock with the Hanbō between the opponent's hip and upper right arm.

5. Finally, I step back with my right foot and drop to my right knee to pin the opponent to the ground with the lock.

霞掛 Kasumi Gake: Applying a lock between the front of the opponent's hip and their tricep. Also known as Tsuke-Iri.

行違 Iki Chigai

I am in Kata-Yaburi no Kamae.

1. The opponent and I walk towards each other.
2. As the opponent passes me to my right, he suddenly draws a concealed Shōtō and cuts at my right side.
3. I evade by stepping to my left with my left foot, facing my opponent, and raising the right end of the Hanbō to my right shoulder with my right hand. Then, I slide the left end of the stick up to strike the opponent's right hand from below, knocking the blade from their grip.
4. Finally, I step diagonally to my left with my left foot, release my left hand, and swing the left end of the stick around in a big arc to strike at the opponent's face.

顔砕 Kao Kudaki

I am in Kata-Yaburi no Kamae.

1. The opponent attacks with a right-hand stab at my stomach with a Shōtō.

2. I step to my left with my left foot, turn my body, and slide the right end of the Hanbō up to strike at the opponent's right hand from below, knocking the blade from their grip.
3. I then release my left hand and swing the left end of the stick around in a big arc to strike at the opponent's face.

当返し Ate Gaeshi

I am in Kata-Yaburi no Kamae.

1. The opponent cuts down from Daijōdan no Kamae with a Shōtō.
2. At the moment the opponent initiates their attack, I simultaneously step in with my right foot, drop to my left knee and release my left hand to turn the Hanbō over to thrust to the opponent's solar plexus with the end of the stick.

逆落し Gyaku Otoshi

I am in Kata-Yaburi no Kamae.

1. The opponent attacks with a right-hand stab at my chest with a Shōtō.
2. I step diagonally forward with my left foot and raise the Hanbō with both hands to shoulder level, parrying the attack from below the opponent's right elbow with the middle of the stick.
3. I then leap around behind the opponent as I slide the stick through my hands, in front of the opponent's neck, so that my left hand is in the middle of the stick.
4. I release my right hand to grasp the left end of the stick with my right, encircle the opponent's neck, and apply a choke.
5. Finally, I turn to my right as I maintain the choke and drop my hips to lift the opponent onto my back before dropping them with Gyaku-Otoshi*.

---

* 逆落し Gyaku Otoshi: "Rear Drop"

逆落し *Gyaku Otoshi*

[Note: For safety in training, it is only necessary to rotate the hips in without lifting the opponent onto your back and applying the throw.]

CHAPTER 6
HANBŌ: CHŪDEN NO KATA
中傳之型

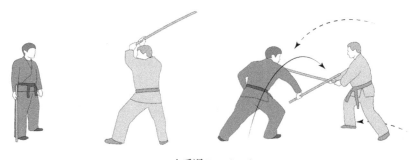

小手返 *Kote Gaeshi*

小手返 Kote Gaeshi

I hold the Hanbō in my right hand in Munen-Musō no Kamae, while the opponent holds a Daitō* in Daijōdan no Kamae.

1. The opponent cuts down at the top of my head.
2. I evade to my right, turn my body, and swing the rear end of the Hanbō over in a big arc to strike down at the opponent's wrists.

---

* 大刀 Daitō: long sword

逆落 Gyaku Otoshi

I hold the Hanbō in my right hand in Munen-Musō no Kamae, while the opponent holds a Daitō in Daijōdan no Kamae.

1. The opponent cuts down at the top of my head.
2. I step to my left with my left foot, evading to my left, as I swing the Hanbō around clockwise in a big arc with my right hand to strike at the right side of the opponent's head.

拂技 Harai Waza

I hold the Hanbō in my right hand in Munen-Musō no Kamae.

1. The opponent cuts down from Daijōdan no Kamae with a Daitō.
2. I step forward with my right foot and swing the Hanbō upward to strike under the opponent's left wrist.
3. I step to my left and swing the Hanbō around clockwise in a big arc to strike at the right side of the opponent's head.

外輪 Soto Wa

I hold the Hanbō in my right hand in Munen-Musō no Kamae.

1. The opponent switches their posture with the Daitō from Daijōdan no Kamae to Seigan no Kamae, then attacks with a straight thrust at my chest.
2. I step to my right with my right foot and swing the Hanbō around anti-clockwise in a big arc to strike at the opponent's upper arm from above.
3. I bring the left end of the Hanbō up to my left hand, grasp it, and slide the stick through my right hand to thrust it at the opponent's solar plexus.

CHAPTER 7

HANBŌ: OKUDEN NO KATA

奥傳之型

一刀 Ittō

一刀 Ittō

I am in Otonashi no Kamae.

1. The opponent cuts down from Daijōdan no Kamae with a Daitō*.
2. I step to my right with my right foot and drop to my left knee as I release my left hand and swing the Hanbō up to strike at the opponent's wrists from below.

_____

* 大刀 Daitō: long sword

返倒 **Hentō**

I am in Otonashi no Kamae.

1. The opponent cuts down from Daijōdan no Kamae with a Daitō.
2. I step to my right with my right foot and drop to my left knee as I release my left hand and swing the Hanbō up to strike at the opponent's wrists from below.
3. With my right hand, I swing the Hanbō around clockwise in a big arc to strike at the opponent's left knee.

跳落し *Hane Otoshi*

跳落し **Hane Otoshi**

I am in Otonashi no Kamae.

1. The opponent cuts down from Daijōdan no Kamae with a Daitō.

2. I step to my left with my left foot while rolling the right end of the Hanbō over my right shoulder with my right hand (while maintaining my right-hand grip on the Hanbō).
3. I then strike down to the opponent's arms from above with the left end of the Hanbō.

股掛け Mata Kake

I am in Otonashi no Kamae.

1. The opponent cuts down from Daijōdan no Kamae with a Daitō.
2. I step to my left with my left foot, release my left hand and swing the left end of the Hanbō up to strike at the opponent's wrists from below.
3. I then turn my right wrist as I swing the Hanbō around clockwise in a big arc to strike up at the opponent's groin from below.

小手拂 Kote Barai

I am in Otonashi no Kamae.

1. The opponent switches their posture with the Daitō from Daijōdan no Kamae to Seigan no Kamae, then attacks with a straight thrust at my chest.
2. I step to my left with my left foot while rolling the right end of the Hanbō over my right shoulder with my right hand (while maintaining my right-hand grip on the Hanbō).
3. I release my left hand and swing the rear end of the Hanbō over in a big arc to strike down at the opponent's wrists from above.
4. I then turn my right wrist as I swing the Hanbō around clockwise in a big arc to strike at the opponent's face.

PART II
ROKUSHAKU-BŌJUTSU

六尺棒術

CHAPTER 8

ROKUSHAKU-BŌ (LONG STAFF)

六尺棒

The Keiko Gata* of the Kukishin Ryū forms the basis of our Rokushaku-Bōjutsu, which can then be expanded to incorporate the essence of all the Ryūha† that make up the Bujinkan. Rokushaku-Bōjutsu includes not only strikes and thrusts but also, when integrated with Taijutsu, includes Gyaku-Waza‡, Nage-Waza§ and Shime-Waza#.

Most of the Rokushaku-Bō Kata are designed for combat against an opponent armed with a sword. The length of the Bō is used to maintain distance while delivering a continuous barrage of strikes, sweeps, and thrusts with both ends of the staff, keeping the opponent off balance and on the defensive. In Kukishin Ryū, Rokushaku-Bōjutsu provides the foundation for using other long weapons such as Yari (spear) and Naginata (glaive/halberd). Additionally, Kenjutsu is introduced by learning to receive, defend, and counter the Bō with the sword.

Basic handling of the Bō involves rotating it while moving the body left and right. Practice this motion until the staff feels like an extension of your body. The Bō should be held lightly, allowing it to slide freely through

---

* 稽古型 Keiko Gata: practice forms
† 流派 Ryūha: Schools (of Martial Arts)
‡ 逆技 Gyaku-Waza: joint locking techniques
§ 投技 Nage-Waza: throwing techniques
# 絞め技 Shime-Waza: constriction techniques

your hands to effectively utilise its weight. Synchronised body movements seamlessly transfer power through the Bō via the coordinated action of the foot, spine, hand, and Bō, delivering maximum force through the weapon.

Additionally, either end of the Bō can thrust at the opponent. This can be practised by tapping nails at different points on a post and driving each one in with a single thrust of the Bō as you move freely around it.

There is a Kuden* that states;

「棒先で、虚空を突いて、我が手先、手応えあれば、
極意なりけり」
*"Thrust into the air (void); when you feel a response in
your hands - this is Gokui†."*

Hatsumi-sensei has explained that the true meaning of this Kuden is the realisation that, no matter how many times you thrust the Bō into the air, you will never actually feel any resistance in your hands. This highlights that the essence of the technique lies not in the mystical but in straightforward and consistent practice.

Techniques of Rokushaku-Bō also include Nage-Bō (Throwing the Staff). A thrown staff could serve as a distraction as you draw another weapon or even as an attack in its own right.

- 直打法 **Chokudahō (Direct Hit Method)**: The end of the staff is launched directly at the opponent.
- 回転打ち **Kaiten Uchi (Rotating Strike)**: The staff is thrown spinning at the opponent.
- 蹴り打ち **Keri Uchi (Kicking Strike)**: One end of the staff is placed on top of the foot and kicked at the opponent.

---

* 口伝 Kuden: "verbally transferred knowledge"
† 極意 Gokui: Innermost secrets (of an art or skill); mysteries; essence; heart.

History

In 1336, Yakushimaru Kurando, then 16 years old, was tasked by Kusunoki Masahige* of the Southern Court with a daring mission: to rescue Emperor Go-Daigo†, who was imprisoned at the Kazan-in palace by Ashikaga Takauji‡ of the Northern Court.

Disguised as a lady-in-waiting, Kurando infiltrated the palace and managed to escape with the Emperor on his back. Pursuers caught up with them at the Kuragari Tōge Pass, on the border of Nara and Osaka prefectures. There, Kurando valiantly defended himself and the Emperor with his naginata. During the fierce battle, the blade of his naginata was severed, but Kurando continued to fight using the weapon's shaft as a Bō. He held off the attackers until reinforcements from Kusunoki Masashige's troops arrived.

In recognition of his bravery, Emperor Go-Daigo honoured Kurando with the surname Kuki (also pronounced Kukami). The Rokushaku-Bōjutsu techniques of the Kukishin Ryū are based on the methods Kurando employed during this courageous rescue.

Rokushaku-Bō Dimensions

In the Bujinkan, the standard length for the Bō is 6-shaku (181.8cm), which matches the height of the lintel of a traditional Japanese house. The measurement was also viewed as the effective range of a sword.

Rokushaku-Bō can be crafted from any suitable hardwood, with historical preferences being either Akagashi (Japanese Red Oak) or Shirakashi (Japanese White Oak) with a diameter of 1-sun (3cm).

In addition to practising with a wooden stick, a soft training Bō can be fashioned using a conduit core padded with pipe insulation and wrapped in vinyl, leather or cloth duct tape. This soft training tool allows you to strike

---

* 楠木正成 Kusunoki Masashige (1294 - 1336): Famous military leader who supported the revolt to restore Imperial power.
† 後醍醐天皇 Emperor Go-Daigo (1288 - 1339): 96th emperor of Japan.
‡ 足利尊氏 Ashikaga Takauji (1305-1358): first Shogun of the Ashikaga shogunate.

through your target and commit to the techniques while providing a higher level of safety.

Other Types of Bō

In the Bujinkan, training extends beyond the standard Rokushaku-Bō to include a variety of other staff types. Each staff differs in length, shape, and weight, necessitating unique techniques tailored to these characteristics.

While there are no formal Kata for these alternative Bō, practitioners master their use through direct instruction from their teacher (Kuden) and by creatively adapting traditional techniques and applications (Henka).

Various types of longer staffs and different cross-sections include the following:

- 七尺棒 Nanashaku-Bō ("7-shaku (212.7cm) staff")
- 八尺棒 Hashaku-Bō ("8-shaku (242.4cm) staff")
- 九尺棒 Kyushaku-Bō ("9-shaku (272.7cm) staff")
- 八角棒 Hakkaku-Bō ("Octagonal staff")

Additionally, there are specialised Bō, including the following:

鉄輪入六尺棒 Tetsurin-Iri Rokushaku-Bō

A design of Rokushaku-Bōjutsu from the Kukishin Ryū that included nine steel rings fixed to the staff. Four rings at either end are placed 3cm apart, and one ring is placed centrally on the Bō.

鉄輪入六尺棒 Tetsurin-Iri Rokushaku-Bō

呑龍棒 Donryu-Bō

This is a design of Bō from the Kukishin Ryū. Four metal spear-like tips are secured to one end, and nine steel rings with studs, plus a metal tip, are attached to the other. Inside the staff, a weight and chain are concealed.

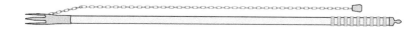

呑龍棒 *Donryu-Bō*

大車輪棒 Dai Sharin-Bō

An 8-shaku-long Bō with a wheel attached to either end.

大車輪棒 *Dai Sharin-Bō*

如意棒 Nyoibo

A very heavy staff/club, sometimes plated or studded with steel.

如意棒 *Nyoibo*

仕込み杖 Shikomi-Bō

A Bō that outwardly appears to be a staff but conceals a sword, knife, weighted chain or other weapon inside the stick.

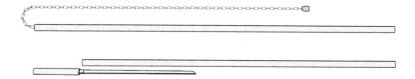

仕込み杖 *Shikomi-Bō*

CHAPTER 9
BŌ: KYŪHŌ NO KAMAE
九法之構

上段の構 Jōdan no Kamae

I hold the Bō in the centre with both hands shoulder-width apart. My right hand is raised above my head, and my left hand is held out in front. My left foot is in front, and my right foot is behind.

上段の構 Jōdan no Kamae

中段の構 Chūdan no Kamae

I hold the Bō in the centre with both hands shoulder-width apart. My left hand is held straight out, and my right hand is at the right-hand side of the chest. My left foot is in front, and my right foot is behind.

中段の構 *Chūdan no Kamae*

下段の構 Gedan no Kamae

I hold the Bō at the left end with both hands shoulder-width apart. The right end of the Bō rests on the ground. My left foot is in front, and my right foot is behind.

下段の構 *Gedan no Kamae*

一文字の構 Ichimonji no Kamae

I hold the Bō at the centre with both hands, palms facing downward, shoulder-width apart. The staff is held horizontally. My left foot is in front, and my right foot is behind.

一文字の構 *Ichimonji no Kamae*

平一文字の構 Hira Ichimonji no Kamae

I hold the Bō at the centre with both hands, palms facing downward, shoulder-width apart. My body faces directly forward, and the staff is held horizontally.

平一文字の構 *Hira Ichimonji no Kamae*

諰変の構 Ihen no Kamae

I hold the Bō at the centre with both hands shoulder-width apart. My left hand is held straight out, and my right hand is near to the side of my head. My left foot is in front, and my right foot is behind.

[Note: Ihen no Kamae is about adopting a changeable and adaptive posture. It can be varied by raising the right hand and dropping the left, changing the grips or holding the Bō behind you in a Kamae similar to Heitō no Kamae]

諂変の構 *Ihen no Kamae*

請願の構 Seigan no Kamae

I hold the Bō with my right hand facing to my left and my left hand facing to my right. My left hand is at my waist, and my right hand is held in front of me. My right foot is in front, and my left foot is behind.

請願の構 *Seigan no Kamae*

天地人の構 Tenchijin no Kamae

I hold the Bō vertically, with my right hand facing to my left and my left hand facing to my right. My right hand sits under my jaw, with my elbow rounded and my left hand held at my body. My left foot is in front, and my right foot is a small step behind. My body is in a half-facing posture.

天地人の構 *Tenchijin no Kamae*

撃倒の構 Heitō no Kamae

I hold the Bō at the left end with both hands, palms facing downward, shoulder-width apart. The right end of the Bō is pulled back behind me so that it sits on the ground to my left side. My left foot is in front, and my right foot is behind.

撃倒の構 *Heitō no Kamae*

CHAPTER 10
BŌ: BŌ NO SAHŌ (ETIQUETTE)
棒之行法

Prior to paired practice in Rokushaku-Bōjutsu, respect is expressed towards your training partner with the following traditional ceremony.

棒之行法 Bō no Sahō

1. My training partner and I walk towards each other, holding our Bō horizontally at the centre in our left hands until we are 6 shaku (181.8cm) apart.

2. Keeping our Bō level and in sync, we pass our Bō from our left to our right hands directly in front of us, ensuring the Bō are kept at the same height and angle.

3. We both take a small step back with our left foot as we kneel on our left knees while keeping our Bō level.

4. We then bring our right feet back to kneel on our right knees in the same manner as we carefully place our Bō on the floor to our right side.

5. We raise our weight slightly off our heels and place the insteps on the ground with the feet side by side in Seiza (formal sitting position).

6. From this position, we place our hands on the floor in front with our elbows out and bend our upper body forward while keeping our backs straight for Za-Rei (seated bow).

7. We quickly rise to stand on our right feet, simultaneously grasping the centre of our Bō with our right hands to hold them upright and in line with the outside of our lower right legs.

8. Both my training partner and I say together, "Ote Yawaraka Ni"* ("Let's have safe training"). We then simultaneously slide our right hands down the shaft of our Bō to strike the ground firmly in front of us.

9. We immediately step back with our right feet as we pick up the Bō with our right hands to stand up in Ichimonji no Kamae.

10. We then begin training.

---

* お手やわらかに Ote Yawaraka Ni: (lit. "[Train] softly / gently").

CHAPTER 11
BŌ: KIHON GATA
基本型

受身 Ukemi (Receiving / Parry)

1. My opponent and I face each other with Bō held in Hira Ichimonji no Kamae, standing about 4-shaku (121.2cm) apart.

2. The opponent steps forward with their right foot and strikes downwards to the top of my head with the right end of their Bō. I step back with my right foot to receive the attack.

3. My left hand is held straight up above my head on the left side. My right hand is held just above my head, cradling the Bō in my palm. My right arm is bent with the elbow toward the right end of the Bō. I receive the opponent's Bō in a diagonal position as it strikes down at me.

Ukemi (also called Jodan Uke), shown from the front.

4. We repeat the technique on the opposite side.

The body must be angled to effectively receive an attack, avoiding a direct perpendicular block. The staff should be held so that fingers are not exposed, allowing the opponent's weapon to slide off. The ideal position is where the opponent's weapon grazes the staff and slides down.

足払 Ashi-Barai

1. My opponent and I face each other with Bō held in Hira Ichimonji no Kamae, standing about 4-shaku (121.2cm) apart.

2. The opponent steps forward with their right foot and strikes at my left leg with Ashi-Barai using the right end of their Bō. I simultaneously step back with my left foot and strike with Ashi-Barai (foot sweep) using the right end of my Bō. Both the opponent's and my Bō clash together between us.

3. The opponent and I then release our right hands and rotate our staff to strike with Ashi-Barai using the left end of the Bō, mirroring each other's motion.

4. We repeat the technique on the opposite side.

This basic is described for Ashi Barai but can also be practised with each of the following basic strikes (Refer to "Chapter 18: Jō Kihon Gata" for a description of each strike).

- 面打ち *Men Uchi (Strike to the Top of the Head)*
- 小手打ち *Kote Uchi (Strike to the Wrist)*
- 胴打ち *Dō Uchi (Strike to the Torso)*
- 横面打ち *Yokomen Uchi (Strike to the Side of the Head)*
- 突 *Tsuki (Thrust)*
- 跳上げ *Hane Age (Upward Strike)*

四方棒振型 Shihō Bōfuri Gata

1. From Ichimonji no Kamae, I flip the Bō up with my left hand and rotate it with my right hand. As the Bō turns over, I catch it with my left hand below my right. My right palm is facing up, and my left is facing down.

2. I step forward with my right foot and push down with my left hand to rotate the Bō up and over with my right hand.

3. I catch the Bō with my left hand as it turns over so that both my palms are now facing down, and I then release my right hand as the Bō continues its spin.

4. As the Bō turns over, I catch it with my right hand below my left. My left palm is facing up, and my right is facing down. I step back with my right foot and push down with my right hand to rotate the Bō up and over

with my left hand.

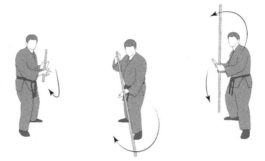

5. I catch the Bō with my right hand as it turns over so my palms face down.

6. I repeat this sequence continuously, causing the Bō to spin to my left and right like a windmill.

Shihō Bōfuri Gata should be practised moving freely and changing direction to the front, sides or back without breaking the rhythm of the spin.

面打ち払い型 Men-Uchi-Harai Gata

In this exercise, the opponent and I mirror each other's motion, with the Bō clashing together in the middle between us.

1. From Ichimonji no Kamae.

2. I flip the Bō up with my left hand…

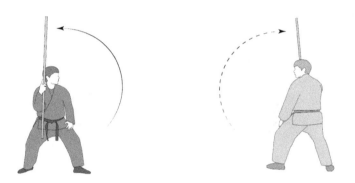

3. … and turn the Bō over to sweep at the opponent's left leg with the right end of the Bō.

4. From this position, I rotate the right end of the Bō to strike at the left side of the opponent's head.

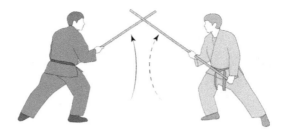

5. I then switch feet and sweep at the opponent's right leg with the left end of the Bō.

6. From this position, I release my right hand and turn the Bō around with my left hand...

7. ...to sweep at the opponent's right leg.

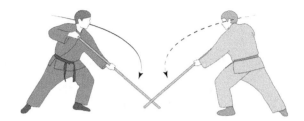

8. We then repeat the technique on the opposite side. Each time, the Bō should clash together between us as we mirror each other's actions exactly.

突き跳ね型 Tsuki Hane Gata

1. My opponent and I face each other with Bō held in Seigan no Kamae.

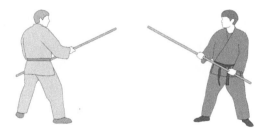

2. I thrust at the opponent with the right end of the Bō. The opponent parries my attack.

3. I step forward with my left foot and rotate the left end of the Bō up and around from below in a big arc, hooking the opponent's weapon from between their hands to break their grip.

4. I step back with my left foot, continuing the rotation of my Bō in a big arc and immediately thrust at the opponent again with the right end of the Bō.

5. I repeat on the opposite side from a Left Seigan no Kamae.

In addition to breaking the opponent's grip, there are numerous variations. If the opponent maintains their grip, the movement can catch their wrist and take them down to the front or rear with Omote / Ura Gyaku. Additionally, the rear end of the Bo can be hooked up from below to strip the opponent of their sword or other weapon.

CHAPTER 12
BŌ: SABAKI GATA
捌型

五法 Gohō

Hira-Ichimonji no Kamae

1. I spin the Bō with Shihō Bōfuri* to both sides.
2. Coming off the spin on my right side, I step forward with my right foot to sweep at the opponent's left leg with the right end of the Bō.
3. I then rotate the right end of the Bō in an arc to strike at the left side of the opponent's head.
4. I step back with my right foot and sweep at the opponent's right leg with the left end of the Bō.
5. I release my right hand and rotate the right end of the Bō around to sweep at the opponent's right leg.

---

*   Refer Chapter 11, "Bō: Kihon Gata - Shihō Bōfuri Gata"

五法 Gohō

裏五法 Ura-Gohō

Hira-Ichimonji no Kamae

1. I spin the Bō with Shihō Bōfuri* to both sides.
2. Coming off the spin on my left side, I step back with my right foot and thrust at the opponent's chest with the left end of the Bō.
3. I then step forward with my right foot and strike at the left side of the opponent's head with the right end of the Bō.
4. I step back with my right foot and sweep the left end of the Bō upward at the opponent's right ankle.
5. I step forward with my right foot, release my left hand, and rotate the left end of the Bō around to strike at the left side of the opponent's head.

---

* Refer Chapter 11, "Bō: Kihon Gata - Shihō Bōfuri Gata"

差合 Sashi-Ai

Chūdan no Kamae

1. I thrust the end of the Bō at the opponent.
2. I slide the Bō back behind me, then step forward with my right foot and strike at the left side of the opponent's body with the right end of the Bō.
3. I step back with my right foot as I rotate the left end of the Bō to strike upward at the opponent's groin.

船張 Funa-Bari

Gedan no Kamae

1. I step forward with my right foot to strike the left side of the opponent's body with the right end of the Bō.
2. I then step back with my right foot and strike down at the top of the opponent's head with the left end of the Bō.
3. I step back with my left foot and strike upward with the right end of the Bō.
4. I step forward with my left foot and strike down at the top of the opponent's head with the left end of the Bō.

鶴の一足 Tsuru no Hito-Ashi

Ten Chi Jin no Kamae

1. I step forward with my right foot as I drop to my left knee and strike the Bō flat on the ground, aiming at the top of the opponent's foot.
2. From this position, I sweep at both of the opponent's legs with the right end of the Bō.
3. I then stand up, step back with my right foot, and strike at the right side of the opponent's head with the left end of the Bō.
4. I release my right hand and rotate the Bō over to strike

downwards at the top of the opponent's head with the right end of the Bō.

5. I then step forward with my right foot to strike the left side of the opponent's head with the right end of the Bō.

6. Finally, I release my left hand and rotate the left end of the Bō around to sweep at the opponent's left leg.

鶴の一足 *Tsuru no Hito-Ashi: Stepping forward with my right foot I drop to my left knee and strike the Bō flat on the ground. From this position, I sweep at both of the opponent's legs with the right end of the Bō.*

裏一足 Ri-Issoku

Gedan no Kamae

1. I step forward with my right foot and sweep at the opponent's left ankle with the right end of the Bō.

2. I step back with my right foot and release my left hand, allowing the Bō to swing back. I retake my left-hand grip behind my right hand and sweep at the opponent's right ankle with the left end of the Bō.

3. From this position, I throw the Bō over with my right hand to strike down at the top of the opponent's head with the right end of the Bō.

4. I then step forward with my right foot and strike downward at the top of the opponent's head with the right end of the Bō.

5. From this position, I release my left hand and rotate the Bō

around to strike at the left side of the opponent's head with the left end of the Bō.

6. I release my left hand and rotate the left end of the Bō around from the inside to sweep at the opponent's left leg.
7. Finally, I step back with my right foot and deliver a straight thrust.

裾落 Suso-Otoshi

Chūdan no Kamae

1. I thrust the end of the Bō at the opponent.
2. I release my left hand and rotate the left end of the Bō around as I step forward with my right foot and strike at the left side of the opponent's body.
3. I then step back with my right foot and sweep at the opponent's right leg with the left end of the Bō.
4. From this position, I throw the Bō over with my right hand to strike downward at the top of the opponent's head with the right end of the Bō.
5. Finally, I throw the left end of the Bō up and around with my left hand as I step forward with my right foot and sweep at the opponent's left leg.

裏裾落 Ura Suso-Otoshi

Chūdan no Kamae

1. I thrust the end of the Bō at the opponent.
2. I step forward with my right foot and sweep at the opponent's left ankle with the right end of the Bō.
3. I step back with my right foot and release my left hand, allowing the Bō to swing back. I retake my left-hand grip behind my right hand and sweep at the opponent's right ankle with the left end of the Bō.
4. I repeat to sweep at the opponent's left ankle.
5. I repeat to sweep at the opponent's right ankle.

6. From this position, I throw the Bō over with my right hand to strike at the top of the opponent's head with the right end of the Bō.
7. I slide the Bō back, then deliver a straight thrust at the opponent.

一本杉 Ippon Sugi

Ten Chi Jin no Kamae

1. I drop to my right knee as I strike the Bō down flat on the ground, aiming at the top of the opponent's foot.
2. I stand up, slide the Bō back, step back with my left foot and sweep at the opponent's left leg with the right end of the Bō.
3. From this position, I throw Bō up and around with my left hand to strike at the left side of the opponent's body with the left end of the Bō.
4. I then step forward with my left foot to strike down at the top of the opponent's head with the left end of the Bō.
5. Finally, I pull back one step and throw the right end of the Bō up and over with my right hand to strike down at the top of the opponent's head.

一本杉 Ippon Sugi: Dropping to my right knee as I strike the Bō down flat on the ground, aiming at the top of the opponent's foot. I then stand up, step back with my left foot and sweep at the opponent's left leg with the right end of the Bō.

瀧落 Taki Otoshi

Chūdan no Kamae

1. I thrust the end of the Bō at the opponent.
2. I step forward with my right foot and rotate the Bō from under my left armpit, across my back, and over my right shoulder to strike at the left side of the opponent's head.
3. I step back with my right foot and rotate the Bō from under my right armpit, across my back, and over my left shoulder to strike at the right side of the opponent's head.
4. Finally, I throw the left end of the Bō up with my left hand, rotate the Bō, retake my left-hand grip behind my right hand, step forward with my right foot, and strike at the left side of the opponent's head.

瀧落 *Taki Otoshi: Rotating the Bō from under my left armpit, across my back, and over my right shoulder to strike at the left side of the opponent's head.*

虚空 Kokū

From Chūdan no Kamae, I thrust the end of the Bō at the opponent. The opponent lifts his sword diagonally upwards from right to left to deflect my thrust, then leaps in to cut down at my head.

1. I pull back one step with my right foot, bend my right arm, and lift my left hand high to receive the opponent's downward cut*.

---

* Refer Chapter 11, "Bō: Kihon Gata - Ukemi"

2. I then take a big step back with my left foot as I throw the left end
   of the Bō up and around with my left hand to strike at the left side
   of the opponent's body.
3. From this position, I rotate the Bō to sweep at the opponent's
   left leg.

虚空 *Kokū: Thrusting the end of the Bō at the opponent. The
opponent lifts his sword diagonally upwards from right to left to
deflect my thrust, then leaps in to cut down at my head.*

笠之内 Kasa no Uchi

Seigan no Kamae

1. I step forward with my left foot and strike horizontally to the right side of the opponent's body with the left end of the Bō.
2. I then step back with my left foot and strike horizontally to the left side of the opponent's body with the right end of the Bō.
3. I step forward with my left foot and strike upward at the opponent with the left end of the Bō.

太刀落 Tachi Otoshi

Ichimonji no Kamae

1. The opponent attacks with a downward cut.
2. I pull back one step with my left foot, bend my left arm, and lift my right hand high to receive the opponent's downward cut.*
3. From this position, I slide my left foot back as I strike down at the opponent's hands from above with the right end of the Bō.
4. I then throw the left end of the Bō up and over with my left hand to strike downward at the top of the opponent's head.

払 Harai

Ichimonji no Kamae

1. The opponent attacks with a downward cut.
2. I step back with my left foot and strike down at the opponent's hands from above with the right end of the Bō.
3. I step forward with my left foot and strike up at the opponent's hands from below with the left end of the Bō.

---

* Refer Chapter 11, "Bō: Kihon Gata - Ukemi"

小手附 Kote Tsuki

Chūdan no Kamae

1. I thrust the end of the Bō at the opponent.
2. I slide the Bō back, then step forward with my right foot and strike at the left side of the opponent's body with the right end of the Bō.
3. I then throw the left end of the Bō up and over with my left hand to strike down at the top of the opponent's head.
4. I step back with my right foot and strike up at the opponent's hands from below with the left end of the Bō.

向詰 Mukō Zume

From Ihen no Kamae, I throw the right end of the Bō up and over with my right hand to strike down at the top of the opponent's head. I repeat three times, alternating left and right.

蹴り挙げ Keri Age

From Ihen no Kamae, I repeat the previous technique, Mukō Zume, but repeating five times, alternating left and right. After the fifth repetition, I release my left hand, rotate the Bō, retake my left-hand grip behind my right hand, step forward with my right foot and strike at the left side of the opponent's body with the right end of the Bō.

撃留 Geki Ryū

Hidari (Left) Seigan no Kamae

1. I thrust the end of the Bō at the opponent.
2. I then step forward with my right foot and strike the left side of the opponent's head with the right end of the Bō.
3. I pull my left foot back, release my left hand, rotate the Bō, and deliver a straight thrust at the opponent.

4. I then release my left hand, rotate the Bō from the inside, retake my left-hand grip behind my right hand and strike horizontally at the left side of the opponent's body.

附入 Tsuke Iri

Migi (Right) Seigan no Kamae

1. I thrust the end of the Bō at the opponent.
2. I then step forward with my left foot and strike horizontally at the right side of the opponent's body with the left end of the Bō.
3. I throw the right end of the Bō up and over with my right hand, drop to my right knee, and deliver a straight thrust at the opponent. This position is also known as Wangetsu-Yue no Kamae*.

五輪碎 Gorin Kudaki

Hidari (Left) Ihen no Kamae

1. I spin the Bō and step forward with my right foot to strike horizontally to the left side of the opponent's body.
2. I then spin the Bō as I step forward with my left foot, striking horizontally to the right side of the opponent's body.
3. I repeat multiple times.

天地人 Ten Chi Jin

Ten Chi Jin no Kamae

1. I step forward with my right foot as I rotate the right end of the Bō around to strike upward at the opponent.
2. I then change to quickly pull the Bō back and deliver a straight thrust.

---

* 弯月の構 Wangetsu-Yue no Kamae

3. I step back with my right foot and strike at the right side of the opponent's head with the left end of the Bō.
4. Next, I step forward with my right foot to sweep at the opponent's left leg with the right end of the Bō.
5. Finally, I step back with my right foot, throw the right end of the Bō up and over with my right hand, and deliver a straight thrust at the opponent.

前広 Mae Hiro

Chūdan no Kamae

1. I step forward with my right foot as I strike horizontally at the left side of the opponent's body with the right end of the Bō.
2. I throw the left end of the Bō up and over with my left hand to strike down at the top of the opponent's head.
3. Next, I leap back to Ten Chi Jin no Kamae, drop to my right knee and strike the Bō down flat on the ground, aiming at the top of the opponent's foot, as per the technique Ippon Sugi.
4. With my right knee remaining on the ground, I raise the Bō and deliver a straight thrust at the opponent.

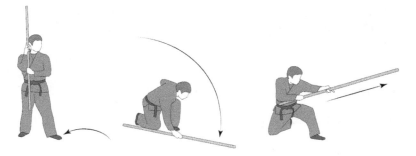

前広 Mae Hiro: Leaping back one step to Ten Chi Jin no Kamae, dropping to my right knee and striking the Bō down flat on the ground, aiming at the top of the opponent's foot. With my right knee remaining on the ground, I raise the Bō and thrust at the opponent.

両小手 Ryō Kote

Chūdan no Kamae

1. I step back with my left foot and strike upward the opponent's hands with the right end of the Bō.
2. I throw the left end of the Bō up and over with my left hand to strike down at the top of the opponent's head.
3. I step forward with my left foot and strike upward at the opponent with the left end of the Bō.
4. I then step back with my left foot and sweep at the opponent's left leg with the right end of the Bō.

浦波 Uranami

Ihen no Kamae

1. I thrust, then quickly pull the Bō back.
2. I throw the rear end of the Bō up and over with my right hand to strike down at the top of the opponent's head from above.
3. I pull the Bō back and thrust.
4. I then rotate the Bō from under my left armpit and around my back to strike horizontally at the left side of the opponent's body.

浦波 Uranami: Rotating the Bō from under my left armpit and around my back to strike horizontally at the left side of the opponent's body.

玉返 Tama Gaeshi

Ihen no Kamae

1. I thrust the end of the Bō at the opponent's face.
2. I then pull the Bō back and step forward with my right foot to strike the left side of the opponent's body with the right end of the Bō.
3. I throw the left end of the Bō up and around with my left hand and thrust it at the left side of the opponent's face.
4. From this position, I rotate the end of the Bō around to sweep at the opponent's left leg.
5. Finally, I step back with my right foot and strike upward at the opponent with the left end of the Bō.

CHAPTER 13
BŌ: SHODEN GATA
初傳型

中段扞技 Chūdan Kangi

Chūdan no Kamae

1. I release my left hand and rotate the left end of the Bō around as I step forward with my right foot and strike at the left side of the opponent's body.
2. I then step back with my right foot and throw the Bō over with my right hand, striking downward at the top of the opponent's head.
3. From this position, I quickly pull the Bō back and deliver a straight thrust.

下段扞技 Gedan Kangi

Gedan no Kamae

1. I step forward with my right foot to sweep at the opponent's left leg with the right end of the Bō.
2. I then rotate the right end of the Bō in an arc to strike at the left side of the opponent's head.

3. I step back with my right foot, switch my grip by releasing my right hand to grasp below my left, and strike at the right side of the opponent's head.
4. From this position, I quickly pull the Bō back and deliver a straight thrust at the opponent's face.

詒変扞技 Ihen Kangi

Ihen no Kamae

1. I release my left hand and rotate the left end of the Bō around as I step forward with my right foot and strike at the left side of the opponent's head.
2. I step back with my right foot and strike upward at the opponent's groin with the left end of the Bō.

上段護技 Jōdan Gogi

Jōdan no Kamae

1. I step forward with my right foot and strike down at the opponent's hands from above with the right end of the Bō.
2. I step back with my right foot and strike upward at the opponent with the left end of the Bō.
3. I step forward with my right foot and strike downward at the top of the opponent's head with the right end of the Bō.

一文字護技 Ichimonji Gogi

Ichimonji no Kamae

1. I circle to my right, quickly thrusting and withdrawing my Bō three times.
2. I then throw the rear end of the Bō up and over with my right hand to strike down at the top of the opponent's head from above.
3. I quickly pull the Bō back and deliver a straight thrust.

平一文字護技 Hira Ichimonji Gogi

Hira Ichimonji no Kamae

1. I step back with my right foot and thrust at the opponent's chest with the left end of the Bō.
2. I step forward with my right foot, switch my grip by releasing my left hand and grasping below my right, and strike downward at the top of the opponent's head.
3. I then release my left hand, rotate the Bō from the inside, retake my left-hand grip behind my right hand and strike horizontally at the left side of the opponent's body.

一文字抛技 Ichimonji Kōgi

Ichimonji no Kamae

1. I throw the right end of the Bō up and over with my right hand to strike at the top of the opponent's head from above. I repeat three times, alternating left and right.
2. After the third repetition, I release my left hand, rotate the Bō, retake my left-hand grip behind my right hand, step forward with my right foot and strike at the left side of the opponent's body with the right end of the Bō.

青眼抛技 Seigan Kōgi

Seigan no Kamae

1. I release my left hand, rotate the Bō from the inside, retake my left-hand grip behind my right hand and strike horizontally at the left side of the opponent's body.
2. I step back with my right foot as I release my left hand, allowing the Bō to swing back. I retake my left-hand grip behind my right hand and sweep at the opponent's right ankle.
3. From this position, I throw the Bō over with my right hand to strike downward at the top of the opponent's head.

天地人抛技 Tenchijin Kōgi

Ten Chi Jin no Kamae

1. I step forward with my right foot and strike at the left side of the opponent's body with the right end of the Bō.
2. From this position, I release my left hand and rotate the left end of the Bō around from below to sweep at the opponent's left leg.
3. I step back with my right foot and strike downward at the top of the opponent's head with the left end of the Bō.

CHAPTER 14
BŌ: CHŪDEN GATA
中傳型

上段挨技 Jōdan Aigi

Jōdan no Kamae

1. I release my left hand and rotate the left end of the Bō as I step forward with my right foot and drop to my left knee to strike upward at the opponent's wrists from below.
2. From this position, I release my left hand and rotate the left end of the Bō around from below to sweep at the opponent's left leg.

下段挨技 Gedan Aigi

Gedan no Kamae

1. I step forward with my right foot and drop to my left knee as I strike downward at the top of the opponent's head with the right end of the Bō.
2. Next, I leap back to Ten Chi Jin no Kamae, drop to my left knee and strike the Bō down flat on the ground, aiming at the top of the opponent's foot.
3. From this position, I sweep at both of the opponent's legs with the right end of the Bō.

平一文字挨技 Hira Ichimonji Aigi

Hira Ichimonji no Kamae

1. I release my left hand and rotate the left end of the Bō around as I step forward with my right foot, drop to my left knee and sweep at the opponent's left leg.
2. From this position, I then rotate the right end of the Bō in an arc to strike at the left side of the opponent's head.
3. I stand up, release my left hand, rotate the left end of the Bō around from the inside and strike at the left side of the opponent's body.

中段擣技 Chūdan Chūgi

Chūdan no Kamae

1. I thrust, then quickly pull the Bō back.
2. I thrust again at the opponent's body.
3. I step forward with my right foot and strike at the left side of the opponent's head with the right end of the Bō.

一文字擣技 Ichimonji Chūgi

Ichimonji no Kamae

1. I step to my right as I thrust the end of the Bō at the opponent.
2. I then rotate the Bō from under my left armpit, across my back, and over my right shoulder to strike at the left side of the opponent's head.

詒変擣技 Ihen Chūgi

Ihen no Kamae

1. I thrust, then quickly pull the Bō back.

2. I step forward with my right foot and strike at the left side of the opponent's body with the right end of the Bō.
3. I step back with my right foot and strike upward at the opponent with the left end of the Bō.
4. From this position, I quickly pull the Bō back and deliver a straight thrust.

青眼摧技 Seigan Saigi

Seigan no Kamae

1. I step back to Ten Chi Jin no Kamae to draw my opponent in, then step forward with my right foot as I strike downward at the top of the opponent's head with the right end of the Bō.
2. From this position, I release my left hand, rotate the Bō from the inside, retake my left-hand grip behind my right hand and strike horizontally at the left side of the opponent's head.
3. I then rotate the right end of the Bō clockwise in a big arc to strike upward at the opponent's groin.

天地人摧技 Tenchijin Saigi

Ten Chi Jin no Kamae

1. I step forward with my right foot as I rotate the right end of the Bō around to strike upward at the opponent.
2. From this position, I release my left hand and rotate the left end of the Bō up from below to strike upward once more at the opponent.
3. I step back with my right foot and deliver a straight thrust at the opponent's body with the left end of the Bō.
4. I then rotate the Bō from under my left armpit and around my back to strike horizontally at the left side of the opponent's head.

一文字摧技 Ichimonji Saigi

Ichimonji no Kamae

1. I spin the Bō with Shihō Bōfuri* to both sides.
2. Coming off the spin on my right side, I step forward with my right foot to strike at the left side of the opponent's body with the right end of the Bō.
3. From this position, I release my left hand, rotate the Bō from the inside, retake my left-hand grip behind my right hand and again strike horizontally at the right side of the opponent's body.
4. Finally, I step back with my right foot, throw the right end of the Bō up and over with my right hand, and deliver a straight thrust at the opponent's body.

---

* Refer Chapter 11, "Bō: Kihon Gata - Shihō Bōfuri Gata"

CHAPTER 15
BŌ: OKUDEN GATA
奥傳型

上段搶技 Jōdan Sōgi

Jōdan no Kamae

1. I throw the right end of the Bō up and over with my right hand to strike downward at the top of the opponent's head.
2. From this position, I pull the Bō back, then deliver a straight thrust at the opponent's body.
3. I step forward with my right foot and strike at the left side of the opponent's head with the right end of the Bō.
4. I then step back with my right foot and deliver a straight thrust at the opponent's body with the left end of the Bō.
5. I pull the Bō back, step to my right and deliver another straight thrust at the opponent's body.

下段搶技 Gedan Sōgi

Gedan no Kamae

1. I throw the right end of the Bō up and over with my right hand to strike downward at the top of the opponent's head.

2. From this position, I pull the Bō back, then deliver a straight thrust at the opponent's body.
3. I pull the Bō back again and deliver another straight thrust at the opponent's body.

平一文字搶技 Hira Ichimonji Sōgi

Hira Ichimonji no Kamae

1. I step back with my left foot and deliver a straight thrust at the opponent's body with the right end of the Bō.
2. I then step back with my right foot as I deliver another straight thrust to the opponent's body with the left end of the Bō.
3. Finally, I drop to my right knee and again deliver a straight thrust at the opponent's body with the left end of the Bō.

中段推技 Chūdan Kakugi

Chūdan no Kamae

1. I thrust, then quickly pull the Bō back.
2. I rotate the Bō from under my left armpit and around my back, step forward with my right foot and sweep at the opponent's left leg.
3. I step back with my right foot and throw the Bō over with my right hand, striking down at the top of the opponent's head.
4. I pull the Bō back and deliver a straight thrust at the opponent's body.

一文字推技 Ichimonji Kakugi

Ichimonji no Kamae

1. I step to my right as I thrust the end of the Bō at the opponent's body.
2. I then rotate the Bō from under my left armpit and around my

back, stepping back with my left foot as I drop to my left knee and strike horizontally at the left side of the opponent's body.

詁変推技 Ihen Kakugi

Ihen no Kamae

1. I throw the right end of the Bō up and over with my right hand to strike downward at the top of the opponent's head.
2. From this position, I pull the Bō back, then deliver a straight thrust at the opponent's body.
3. I step forward with my right foot and strike upward at the opponent's groin with the right end of the Bō.
4. I then rotate the Bō from under my left armpit, across my back, and over my right shoulder to strike at the left side of the opponent's head.

青眼拒技 Seigan Yakugi

Hidari (Left) Seigan no Kamae

1. I step forward with my right foot and strike the left side of the opponent's head with the right end of the Bō.
2. I then throw the left end of the Bō up and over with my left hand to strike downward at the top of the opponent's head.
3. I step back with my right foot as I strike at the right side of the opponent's head with the left end of the Bō.
4. I throw the right end of the Bō up and over with my right hand to strike downward at the top of the opponent's head.
5. I release my right hand and rotate the right end of the Bō around from the inside to strike at the right side of the opponent's head.

天地人拒技 Tenchijin Yakugi

Ten Chi Jin no Kamae

1. I drop to my right knee as I strike the Bō down flat on the ground, aiming at the top of the opponent's foot.
2. With my right knee remaining on the ground, I raise the Bō and thrust at the opponent from this position.
3. I stand up, step forward with my right foot and sweep at the opponent's left leg with the right end of the Bō.
4. From this position, I throw the left end of the Bō up and over with my left hand to strike downward at the top of the opponent's head.

撃倒拒技 Heitō Yakugi

Ten Chi Jin no Kamae

1. I drop to my right knee as I strike the Bō down flat on the ground, aiming at the top of the opponent's foot.
2. I stand up and thrust at the opponent's chest with the left end of the Bō.
3. I then rotate the Bō from under my left armpit and around my back, grasping the right end of the Bo with my right hand (palm facing behind).
4. I roll the right end of the Bō over my right shoulder with my right hand (while maintaining my right-hand grip on the Bō) and strike to the left side of the opponent's head.

撃倒拒技 Heitō Yakugi: Rolling the right end of the Bō over my right shoulder with my right hand (while maintaining my right-hand grip on the Bō).

PART III
JŌJUTSU

杖術

CHAPTER 16

JŌ (WALKING STAFF)

杖

The Jō is a hardwood staff whose length is based on the popular size of the walking staff used by travellers and pilgrims, both samurai and commoners, across Japan.

The Keiko Gata* of the Kukishin Ryū forms the basis for the techniques of Jōjutsu in the Bujinkan. Unlike weapons such as Ken (sword), Yari (spear) or Naginata (glaive/halberd), the Kukishin Ryū utilised the Jō not as a weapon for use in battle but as a tool of self-defence while on a journey.

The Jō is also viewed in the Bujinkan as a symbol of a great master, skilled in many weapons, who has survived to old age and now exclusively relies on their staff for self-defence.

The practice of Bujinkan Jōjutsu begins by repeating all the techniques of Rokushaku-Bōjutsu and Kenjutsu, using the Jō in place of the original weapon. The distinct length of the Jō enables it to serve both as a staff and a Tachi † when wielded. Additionally, there are nine specific Keiko Gata for the Jō from the Kukishin Ryū.

Outside of training in formal technique for Jōjutsu, the tool is often employed within variations of the basic Taijutsu techniques of each Ryūha

---

* 稽古型 Keiko Gata: practice forms
† 太刀 Tachi: long sword

and freestyle movement in Taijutsu practice. The practitioner should arrive at a state in which the Jō is no longer an external object but an extension of their own body, like an old master who is inseparable from their walking staff.

History

Jōjutsu in the Bujinkan has its origins with the Gyōjajō* (also known as a Shakujō†), a staff topped with metal rings traditionally carried by Buddhist monks throughout Asia. This staff had multiple uses: as a walking staff, a noisemaker to announce the monks' presence, an instrument used during chanting, a tool of protection against predatory animals, and self-defence against bandits.

行者杖 *Gyōjajō: mountain ascetic's staff. The style pictured is that carried by the ninja.*

The martial arts using the Gyōjajō originated in India, China, and Korea before arriving in Japan with the introduction of Buddhism in the sixth century. The martial art developed in Japan with the followers of Shugendō‡.

---

* 行者杖 Gyōjajō: Mountain Ascetic's Staff
† 錫杖 Shakujō: Ritual Staff
‡ 修験道 Shugendō: an ascetic mixture of Buddhist and Shintō practice undertaken in mountainous areas.

The Gyōjajō carried by the ninja varies from the standard design in that it has nine rings instead of eight, is decorated with the deity Bishamonten* at the tip and has a heavy, spear-like tip at its base.

Outside the Bujinkan, Jōjutsu developed as a martial art within various schools throughout the Edō Period[†] but came into prominence in Japan with the popularisation of Shintō Musō-ryū Jōjutsu[‡] in the early 20th century.

Jōjutsu was adapted from the Shintō Musō-ryū by the Japanese police force into Keijōjutsu[§] and by the All Japan Kendo Federation into the modern martial art Seitei Jōdō[#]. Jō is also included in the syllabus of Aikidō.

Jō Dimensions

The standard modern length for a Jō is 4-shaku 2-sun 1-bu (127.6cm) with a diameter of 8-bu (2.4cm), as used in the All Japan Kendo Federation Jōdō and other martial arts such as Aikido.

In the Kukishin Ryū, the historically preferred length was 4-shaku 5-sun (136.4cm) with a diameter of 1-sun (3cm). However, many practitioners prefer to customise the length of the Jō to their height, crafting a Jō tailored to measure from the floor to either their armpit or shoulder height.

Jō can be crafted from any suitable hardwood, but historical preferences are for Akagashi (Japanese Red Oak) or Shirakashi (Japanese White Oak). Another style of Jō favoured in the Bujinkan is crafted from a natural stick, such as you may find in the forest, to serve you as a walking stick. The staff's natural bends and gnarls can be used within the flow of Taijutsu to catch against the opponent's limbs.

In addition to practising with a wooden stick, a soft training Jō can be

---

* 毘沙門天 Bishamonten (the Guardian King of the North)
† Edō Period: 1603 to 1868
‡ 神道夢想流 Shintō Musō-ryū: A school of Jojutsu founded by the samurai Musō Gonno-suke in the 17th century.
§ 警杖術 Keijōjutsu: Police Staff Technique
# 制定杖道 Seitei Jōdō: a modern form of Jōdō created by Japanese martial artist Shimizu Takaji.

fashioned using a conduit core padded with pipe insulation and wrapped in vinyl, leather or cloth duct tape. This soft training tool allows you to strike through your target and commit to the techniques while providing a higher level of safety.

CHAPTER 17
JŌ: KAMAE
構え

諭変の構 Ihen no Kamae

I hold the Jō at the centre with both hands shoulder-width apart. My left hand is held in front of me, and my right hand is near the side of my head. My right foot is in front, with my left behind.

諭変の構 Ihen no Kamae

[Note: Ihen no Kamae is about adopting a changeable and adaptive posture. It can be varied by raising the right hand and dropping the left, changing the grips or holding the Jō behind you in a Kamae similar to Heitō no Kamae from Rokushaku-Bōjutsu.]

I can repeat the posture on the opposite side.

下段の構 Gedan no Kamae

I hold the Jō at the left end with both hands, palms facing downward, shoulder-width apart. The right end of the Jō rests on the ground. My left foot is in front, and my right foot is behind.

下段の構 *Gedan no Kamae*

I can repeat the posture on the opposite side.

中段の構 Chūdan no Kamae

I hold the Jō in the centre with both hands shoulder-width apart. My left hand is held out in front of me, and my right hand is at the right-hand side of the chest. My left foot is in front, and my right foot is behind.

中段の構 *Chūdan no Kamae*

I can repeat the posture on the opposite side.

天地人の構 Tenchijin no Kamae

I hold the Jō vertically, with my right hand facing to my left and my left hand facing to my right. My right hand sits under my jaw, with my elbow rounded, and my left hand is at my right side.

天地人の構 *Tenchijin no Kamae*

I can repeat the posture on the opposite side.

一文字の構 Ichimonji no Kamae

I hold the Jō at the centre with both hands, palms facing downward, shoulder-width apart. The staff is held horizontally. My left foot is in front, and my right foot is behind.

一文字の構 *Ichimonji no Kamae*

I can repeat the posture on the opposite side.

請願の構 Seigan no Kamae

I hold the Jō with my right hand facing to my left and my left hand facing to my right. My left hand is at my waist, and my right hand is held in front of me. My right foot is in front, with my left behind.

請願の構 *Seigan no Kamae*

I can repeat the posture on the opposite side.

自然の構 Shizen no Kamae

I stand in a natural posture, holding the Jō vertically like a walking stick.

自然の構 *Shizen no Kamae*

I can repeat the posture on the opposite side.

CHAPTER 18
JŌ: KIHON GATA
基本型

1. 受身 Ukemi (Receiving / Parry)

その一 Sono Ichi (Version #1)

1. From Ichimonji no Kamae, I step back with my left foot, raising my right hand above my head, cradling the Jō in my palm. My left arm is bent with the elbow pointed toward the left end of the Jō to receive the opponent's downward strike in a diagonal position.

2. I repeat the technique on the opposite side.

その二 Sono Ni (Version #2)

1. From Ichimonji no Kamae, I step forward with my right foot, raising my right hand above my head, cradling the Jō in my palm. My left arm is bent with the elbow pointed toward the left end of the Jō to receive the opponent's downward strike in a diagonal position.

2. I repeat the technique on the opposite side.

2. 面打ち Men Uchi (Strike to the Top of the Head)

その一 Sono Ichi (Version #1)

1. From Ichimonji no Kamae, I step forward with my right foot as I slide the Jō through my hands to strike down at the top of the opponent's head with the right end of the Jō.

2. I repeat the technique on the opposite side.

その二 Sono Ni (Version #2)

1. From Ichimonji no Kamae, I throw the right end of the Jō up and over with my right hand to strike down at the top of the opponent's head.

2. I repeat the technique on the opposite side.

3. 小手打ち Kote Uchi (Strike to the Wrist)

その一 Sono Ichi (Version #1)

1. From Ichimonji no Kamae, I step forward with my right foot as I slide the Jō through my hands to strike down at the opponent's wrists with the right end of the Jō.

2. I repeat the technique on the opposite side.

その二 Sono Ni (Version #2)

1. From Ichimonji no Kamae, I throw the right end of the Jō up and over with my right hand to strike down at the opponent's wrists.

2. I repeat the technique on the opposite side.

4. 胴打ち Dō Uchi (Strike to the Torso)

その一 Sono Ichi (Version #1)

1. From Ichimonji no Kamae, I step forward with my right foot as I slide the Jō through my hands to strike horizontally at the left side of the opponent's body with the right end of the Jō.

2. I repeat the technique on the opposite side.

その二 Sono Ni (Version #2)

1. From Ichimonji no Kamae, I step forward with my right foot as I throw the left end of the Jō up and around with my left hand to strike horizontally at the left side of the opponent's body.

2. I repeat the technique on the opposite side.

5. 足払 Ashi Barai (Leg Sweep)

その一 Sono Ichi (Version #1)

1. From Ichimonji no Kamae, I step forward with my right foot as I slide the Jō through my hands to strike at the opponent's left ankle with the right end of the Jō.

2. I repeat the technique on the opposite side.

その二 Sono Ni (Version #2)

1. From Ichimonji no Kamae, I throw the right end of the Jō up and around with my right hand to strike at the opponent's right ankle.

2. I repeat the technique on the opposite side.

6. 横面打ち Yokomen Uchi (Strike to the Side of the Head)

その一 Sono Ichi (Version #1)

1. From Ichimonji no Kamae, I step forward with my right foot as I slide the Jō through my hands to strike horizontally at the left side of the opponent's head with the right end of the Jō.

2. I repeat the technique on the opposite side.

その二 Sono Ni (Version #2)

1. From Ichimonji no Kamae, I step forward with my right foot as I throw the left end of the Jō up and around with my left hand to strike horizontally at the left side of the opponent's head.

2. I repeat the technique on the opposite side.

7. 突 Tsuki (Thrust)

その一 Sono Ichi (Version #1)

1. From Ichimonji no Kamae, I shift forward with my left foot as I slide the Jō through my left hand to thrust straight at the opponent's face with the left end of the Jō.

2. I repeat the technique on the opposite side.

その二 Sono Ni (Version #2)

1. From Ichimonji no Kamae, I throw the right end of the Jō up and over with my right hand. I then slide the Jō through my left hand to thrust straight at the opponent's face.

2. I repeat the technique on the opposite side.

8. 跳上げ Hane Age (Upward Strike)

その一 Sono Ichi (Version #1)

1. From Ichimonji no Kamae, I step forward with my right foot as I slide the Jō through my hands to strike upwards from below with the right end of the Jō.

2. I repeat the technique on the opposite side.

その二 Sono Ni (Version #2)

1. From Ichimonji no Kamae, I step forward with my right foot as I throw the left end of the Jō up and around with my left hand to strike upwards from below.

2. I repeat the technique on the opposite side.

CHAPTER 19
JŌ: KEIKO GATA
稽古型

十文字 Jūmonji

Ihen no Kamae.

1. I swing the Jō in a large, figure-eight motion (Bō-Furi*) three
   times in front of me. On the third swing, I step forward with my
   right foot and strike at the left side of the opponent's head with
   the right end of the Jō.
2. I then rotate the right end of the Jō around in an arc to strike at the
   left side of the opponent's body.
3. I step back with my right foot and strike at the right side of the
   opponent's head with the left end of the Jō.
4. From this position, I turn the Jō around by bringing my right hand
   forward and the left hand to my right armpit to strike at the right
   side of the opponent's head with the right end of the Jō.
5. Finally, I step forward with my right foot, release my left hand,
   and turn the left end of the Jō around to strike at the left side of
   the opponent's head.

---

* 棒振り Bō-Furi

十文字 *Jūmonji*

六法 Roppō

Gedan no Kamae.

1. I step forward with my right foot as I rotate my body to sweep at the opponent's left leg with the right end of the Jō.
2. I release my right hand, swing the Jō onto my left shoulder, rotate it over my right shoulder, grasp the right end of the Jō with my right hand, release my left hand, and strike at the left side of the opponent's head.
3. I step back with my right foot, throw the right end of the Jō up and over with my right hand, and deliver a straight thrust.

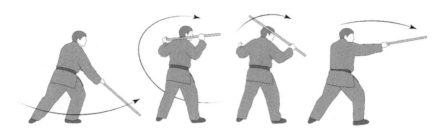

六法 Roppō: Swinging the Jō onto my left shoulder, rotating it over my right shoulder, and striking at the left side of the opponent's head.

九法 Kyūhō

Chūdan no Kamae

1. I strike upwards from my lower right side with the right end of the Jō.
2. I pull my left foot back as I rotate the right end of the Jō around in an arc to strike at the left side of the opponent's head.
3. I step back with my right foot and strike down at the top of the opponent's head with the left end of the Jō.
4. I strike upwards with the right end of the Jō.

5. I rotate the right end of the Jō in an arc to sweep at the opponent's left leg.
6. I step back with my right foot, throw the right end of the Jō up and over with my right hand, and deliver a straight thrust.

飛龍 Hiryū

Ten Chi Jin no Kamae.

1. I step forward with my right foot to strike down at the opponent's left shoulder with the right end of the Jō.
2. I step back with my right foot as I strike down at the top of the opponent's head with the left end of the Jō.
3. I throw the right end of the Jō up and over with my right hand to strike down at the top of the opponent's head.
4. I step back with my left foot and strike horizontally at the left side of the opponent's body with the right end of the Jō.
5. I step forward with my left foot as I strike upwards with the left end of the Jō.
6. I step back with my left foot and strike at the left side of the opponent's head with the right end of the Jō.
7. I step forward with my left foot as I sweep at the opponent's right ankle with the left end of the Jō.
8. I step back with my left foot as I strike horizontally at the left side of the opponent's body with the right end of the Jō.

附入 Tsuke-Iri

Chūdan no Kamae.

1. I thrust straight at the opponent's face with the end of the Jō.
2. I step forward with my right foot as I strike up at the opponent's hands from below with the right end of the Jō.
3. I release my left hand and turn the left end of the Jō around to strike horizontally at the left side of the opponent's body.
4. From this position, I release my left hand and turn the Jō from the

inside to again strike at the left side of the opponent's body with the left end of the Jō.

附入 *Tsuke-Iri: Striking at the left side of the opponent's body, then releasing my left hand and turning the Jō from the inside to strike again at the left side of the opponent's body.*

霞掛 Kasumi Gake

Chūdan no Kamae.

1. I step back, release my left hand, and rotate the left end of the Jō around to strike at the left side of the opponent's head.
2. I release my left hand and rotate the left end of the Bō around to strike again at the left side of the opponent's head.
3. I repeat this three times, finishing with a downward strike at the top of the opponent's head.

腕掛 Ude Kake

Ichimonji no Kamae.

1. The opponent cuts down from Daijōdan no Kamae.
2. I pull back one step with my left foot while bending my left arm and lifting my right hand high to receive the opponent's downward cut with Ukemi*.

---

* Refer Chapter 18: Kihon Gata - Ukemi.

3. I release my left hand and turn the Jō over to strike down at the opponent's arms.

腕掛 *Ude Kake*

小手返 Kote Gaeshi

Seigan no Kamae.

1. I feign (Kyo*) a straight thrust with the end of the Jō.
2. In actuality (Jitsu†), I turn my wrists to strike horizontally at the right side of the opponent's body with the right end of the Jō.

小手返 *Kote Gaeshi*

太刀落 Tachi Otoshi

Seigan no Kamae.

---

* 虚 Kyo: Falsehood/Deception
† 実 Jitsu: Truth

1. The opponent lifts his sword to Daijōdan no Kamae; I also lift my Jō to Daijōdan no Kamae. As the opponent cuts down at the top of my head, I step forward with my right foot as if to strike down to the top of his head.
2. Just before our weapons make contact, I pull the Jō back short with my left hand to strike down at the opponent's wrists.
3. I then drop to my left knee, release my left hand, and rotate the Jō with my right hand to strike upwards from below with the left end of the Jō at the opponent's hands.

太刀落 *Tachi Otoshi*

SELECTED BIBLIOGRAPHY

Hatsumi, M. (2018), *Ninjutsu Kyōden: Bukijutsu.* Tokyo: BAB Japan.

Hatsumi, M. (2014), *The Complete Ninja: The Secret World Revealed.* Tokyo: Kodansha.

Hatsumi, M. (2013), *Ninpo Taizen* Tokyo: Kodansha.

Hatsumi, M. (2005), *Advanced Stick Fighting.* Tokyo: Kodansha.

Hatsumi, M. (1986), *Bōjutsu.* Tokyo: Tsuchiya Shoten

Hatsumi, M. (1983), *Hanbō / Jutte / Tessen.* Tokyo: Tsuchiya Shoten

Hatsumi, M. (1981), *Ninjutsu - History and Tradition.* Burbank, CA. Unique Publications

Hatsumi, M. and Chambers, Q. (1971), *Stick Fighting - Techniques of Self-Defence.* Tokyo: Kodansha

ACKNOWLEDGMENTS

I wish to thank the teachers and senior students of the Bujinkan, under whose personal guidance I gained insight into Budō Taijutsu. In particular, I wish to acknowledge the Bujinkan Sōke (grandmaster), Masaaki Hatsumi-sensei, for his dedication to passing on his legacy to myself and the many thousands of practitioners worldwide.

Special thanks must go to my teacher and mentor, Isamu Shiraishi-sensei, who tirelessly and personally guided my Budō's development over several decades—always with a smile on his face.

I would also like to mention the many other teachers, senior students, and mentors in Japan whose patient guidance, instruction, and friendship over the many years have made my life so much richer.

Thank you to Benjamin Duester, Nathan Anning, and Dale Heers, who have given me suggestions, revisions, notes, and advice throughout this project, and to many of the other prereaders of the manuscript in its various forms for their time and for providing feedback.

Thank you to Nathan Anning and Nathan Kelly for posing for the illustrations.

I also give special thanks to my wife, Yoshie, who has supported me throughout this project.

Finally, I wish to acknowledge the many students of Bujinkan Dōjō Budō Taijutsu worldwide. It is your collective dedication and commitment to this art that ensures its continuation and passing on to future generations.

Duncan Mitchell,

Brisbane, Australia

ABOUT THE AUTHOR

Duncan Mitchell has dedicated over thirty-five years to the study and practice of Bujinkan Dōjō Budō Taijutsu and has been an instructor since 1995. As the founder of Bujinkan Brisbane, Duncan has been conducting martial arts classes in Brisbane since 1997, organising seminars for visiting senior instructors, and hosting several large training events.

From 1990 to 1995, Duncan lived and trained in Japan, studying directly under the grandmaster Masaaki Hatsumi-sensei, senior Bujinkan instructor Isamu Shiraishi-sensei, and many other esteemed Bujinkan teachers. Duncan continues to return to Japan annually to further studies in the martial arts.

Professionally, Duncan has worked as a bridge draftsperson in both Japan and Australia and currently resides in Brisbane. In 2020, Duncan published the first book, "Budo Taijutsu - An Illustrated Reference Guide of Bujinkan Dojo Budo Taijutsu." This publication is Duncan's second book.

Duncan Mitchell can be contacted via email at budodokokai@gmail.com, through the website at www.budodokokai.com, or on the social media platforms listed below.

facebook.com/budodokokai

instagram.com/budodokokai

threads.net/@budodokokai

youtube.com/@budodokokai

ALSO BY DUNCAN MITCHELL

Budo Taijutsu: An Illustrated Reference Guide of Bujinkan Dojo Budo Taijutsu

Printed in the USA
CPSIA information can be obtained
at www.ICGtesting.com
LVHW011648111124
796324LV00042B/927